CORPUS OF MAYA

HIEROGLYPHIC INSCRIPTIONS

VOLUME 2   PART 3   IXKUN
UCANAL
IXTUTZ
NARANJO

CORPUS

OF

MAYA

HIEROGLYPHIC

INSCRIPTIONS

Volume 2   Part 3

IAN GRAHAM

Assistant Curator
of Maya Hieroglyphics
Peabody Museum, Harvard University

PEABODY MUSEUM

OF ARCHÆOLOGY AND ETHNOLOGY

HARVARD UNIVERSITY

CAMBRIDGE, MASSACHUSETTS

1980

ACKNOWLEDGMENTS

Publication of this fascicle was made possible through the generosity of:

    Mrs. Katherine Benedict

    Mrs. Edmund B. Jackson

    Mrs. A. Murray Vaughan

Grateful acknowledgment is made to the Instituto de Antropología e Historia of Guatemala for their cooperation in authorizing fieldwork at the sites described in this fascicle. Part of the fieldwork and preparation of the text were carried out under a three-year grant from the National Endowment for the Humanities, and with matching funds from the Stella and Charles Guttman Foundation of New York and from the Bowditch Exploration Fund of the Peabody Museum.

As this book goes to press, the following volumes of the *Corpus of Maya Hieroglyphic Inscriptions* are available from the Peabody Museum, Harvard University, 11 Divinity Avenue, Cambridge, MA 02138

Ixkun

LOCATION AND ACCESS

Ixkun lies some 9 km north of Dolores, a long-established town in southeastern Peten. The trail from Dolores to the ruins threads through narrow valleys among karst hills for nearly 5 km until it crosses a saddle between hills; thereafter it passes through a basin of flat terrain surrounded by hills. Near the middle of this basin stands the isolated hill that is seen on the site plan as the locus of Structures 26 to 31.

PRINCIPAL INVESTIGATIONS AT THE SITE

The first published notice of the site resulted from the visit of Colonel Modesto Méndez, the Corregidor of Peten, accompanied by the artist Eusebio Lara in 1852. Copies of most of Lara's drawings were published in a German journal in the following year (Ritter 1853), among them drawings from the sites "Yxkun" and "Yxtutz." Blom (1940) correctly identified numbers 10 and 11 of those drawings as Ixkun Stelae 1 and 4, although he was mistaken in seeing number 12 as Stela 5. Lara's drawing of Stela 5 is, however, to be found among the set of pen and wash drawings — probably Lara's originals — that are in the library of the Society of Antiquaries of London.

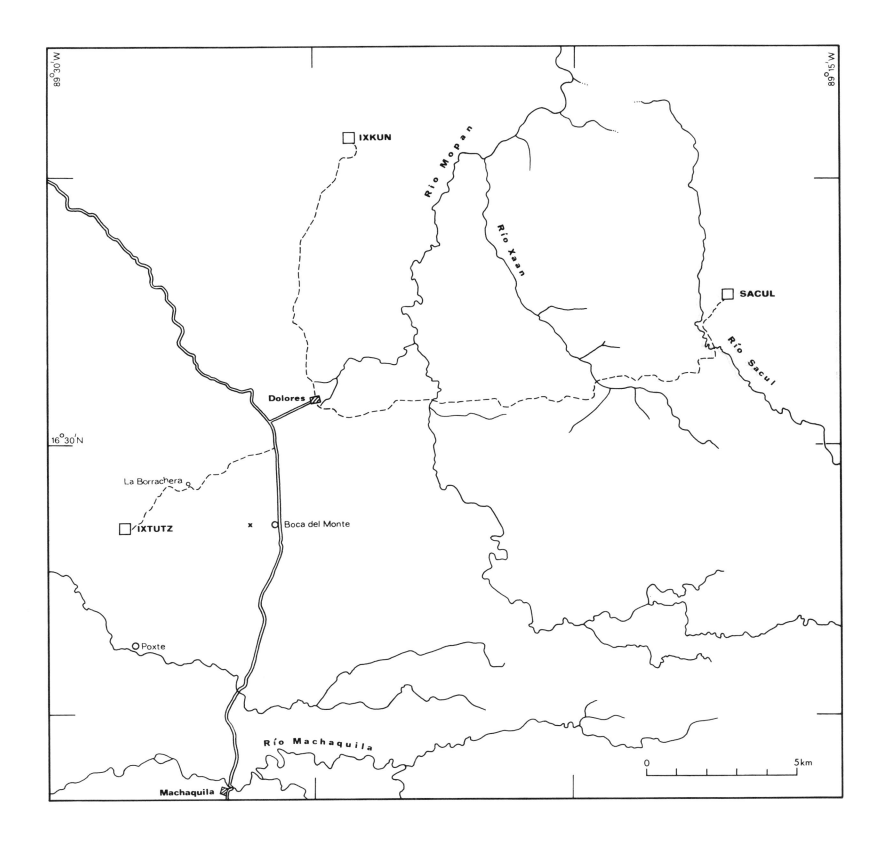

Alfred Maudslay, who had been told of the site in Flores, succeeded in finding it in 1887. He then spent three weeks clearing the site, mapping it, and making a mold of Stela 1; he also cleared rubble from the top of Structure 6, so as to establish the plan of the building. Maudslay published Stela 1 and his plan of the site in his *Biologia* (Maudslay 1889–1902, vol. 2, pls. 67–69) and in *A Glimpse at Guatemala* (Maudslay and Maudslay 1899, pp. 174–176).

In April 1914, Sylvanus G. Morley and Herbert J. Spinden spent three days at Ixkun, photographing the stelae and taking notes on the inscriptions.

My own visits to the site were made in 1971, 1972, and 1978, the first in the company of Eric von Euw, the second prompted by a rumor of damage done by looters to Stela 5. The rumor proved to be only too true: The stela had been wrecked no more than three weeks earlier.

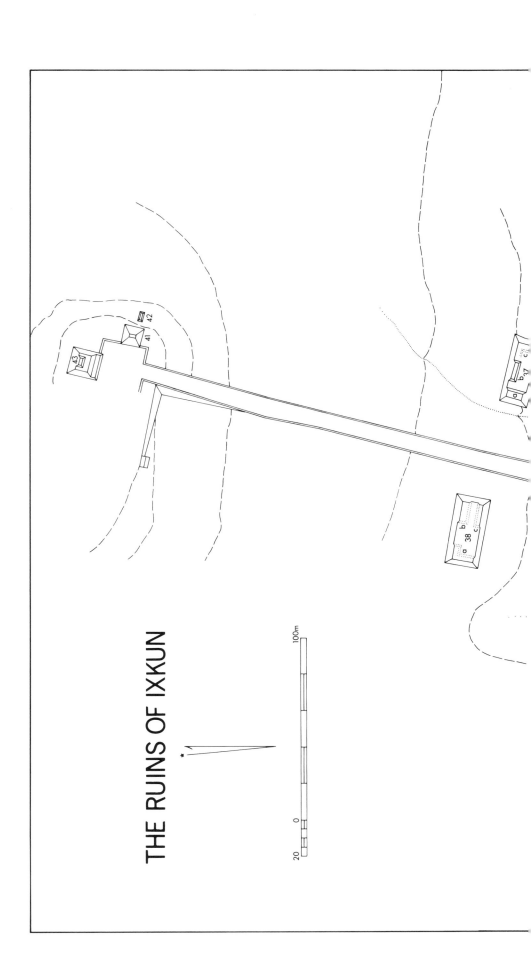

THE RUINS OF IXKUN

NOTES ON THE RUINS   The heart of this ceremonial center consists of two plazas oriented some 10 degrees west of north. The plaza farther to the north is dominated by Structures 3 and 6, which measure 15 m and 11 m high respectively. In this plaza, in addition to the carved stelae described in this volume, there are the standing Stela 10, a poorly trimmed shaft 0.60 m wide, 0.38 m thick, and now only 0.90 m high, and, lying broken on the ground, the remains of Stela 11, also apparently uncarved. In the area between the two plazas the plain Stela 8 still stands, 2.75 m high, 2.58 m wide, and 0.42 m thick.

The larger, southern plaza is defined on its north side by a ball court, and on its west by an acropolis containing an elevated court. This acropolis was evidently raised upon a natural eminence, as attested by rock outcroppings on its northern edge. Structures 20 and 21 rise about 10 m above plaza level.

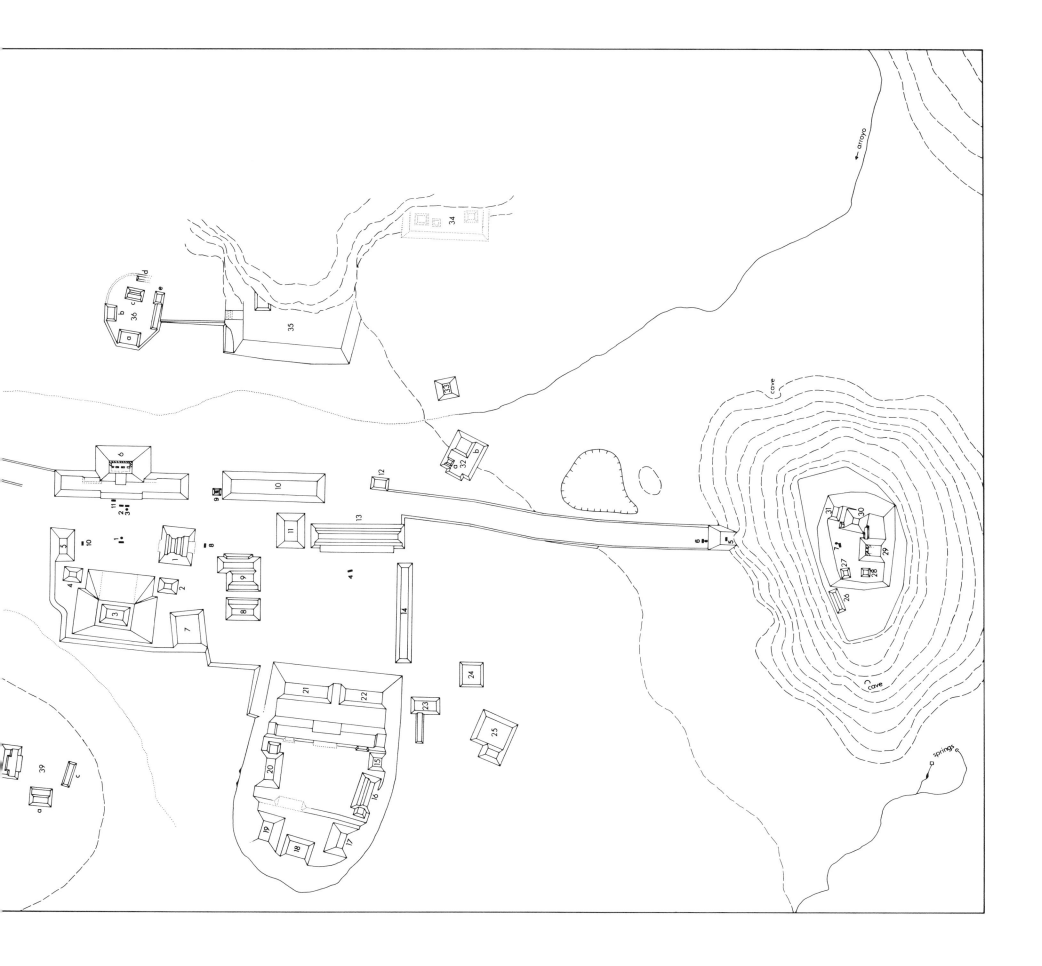

From this central area two causeways run in directions some 20 degrees east of north and 10 degrees west of south. Both causeways are edged with low masonry walls. The southern causeway terminates at a platform 6 m high built against the foot of a hill. Upon this platform stood Stela 5; at the foot of the platform is an oval altar 1.17 m by 0.98 m across, 0.24 m in thickness. On the north side of the altar can be seen the stump and fragments of a stela which show faint signs of carving.

Up the hill, 41 m above this altar, is a terrace, upon which stands a small acropolis, its floor about 6 m above the terrace. The principal edifice, Structure 29, rising 6 m from the floor of the acropolis, has a doorway 1.3 m wide spanned by a lintel which is still in place, although the building is otherwise in ruins. Stela 7, still standing in front of it though inclined sharply forward, is an unsculptured shaft of stone very similar to that of Stela 5. It is 0.52 m wide, 0.18 m thick, with 1.6 m of exposed height. The associated altar is an oval 1.05 m by 0.97 m across. A cave on the west side of the hill (marked on the plan) penetrates some way into the hill and contains the remains of ancient masonry and potsherds, which were not closely examined or recorded.

The arroyo that flows into the southeast corner of the area covered by the site plan is said to fail very seldom, although during the dry season the entire flow sinks into the stream bed as it approaches the hill mentioned above and seems to pass beneath it. At the back of the nearby cave water can be drawn, coming presumably from this source, and on the opposite side of the hill there are two springs, one of them enlarged in antiquity into a rectangular pool 1.9 m by 1.3 m with a border of cut stone. During the rainy season the area on either side of the arroyo near Structures 32 and 33 is liable to flooding.

NOTES ON THE PLAN OF THE SITE

The survey from which the site plan is drawn was begun by von Euw in 1971, and finished by Graham in 1978. Structure 34, missed by us, is copied from Maudslay's plan, which can now be appreciated for its impressive completeness and accuracy. The absence of the ball court from his plan as reproduced in the *Biologia,* and from Morley's version (1937–38, vol. 5, pl. 196) which was based upon it, may be attributed to an error by Maudslay in copying from his original, as reproduced in *A Glimpse at Guatemala* (p. 174). The monument that Morley tentatively labeled Y on his plan owes its origin to a smudge on the lithographic plate in the *Biologia*.

REGISTER OF INSCRIPTIONS AT IXKUN

Stelae 1-5
Altar of Stela 3

REFERENCES CITED

BLOM, FRANS
  1940   "Coronel Modesto Méndez," *Anales de la Sociedad de Geografía e Historia de Guatemala,* vol. 16, pp. 167–179. Guatemala City.
MAUDSLAY, ALFRED P.
  1889-1902   *Biologia Centrali-Americana: Archaeology,* 5 vols. London.
MAUDSLAY, ALFRED P., and ANNE CARY MAUDSLAY
  1899   *A Glimpse at Guatemala.* London.
MORLEY, SYLVANUS G.
  1937-38   *The Inscriptions of Peten.* Carnegie Institution of Washington, Publication 437, 5 vols. Washington, D.C.
RITTER, CARL
  1853   "Ueber neue Entdeckungen und Beobachtungen in Guatemala und Yucatan," *Zeitschrift,* Gesellschaft für Erdkunde zu Berlin, vol. 1, pp. 161–193. Berlin.

Ixkun, Stela 1

LOCATION   This impressive stela stands near the center of the main plaza, in front of Structure 3. The associated altar is circular, 2.05 m in diameter, and 0.35 m thick.

CONDITION   Intact and erect. The surface shows some loss of detail through weathering. Saw cuts at the top testify to an attempt, fortunately soon abandoned, to cut off the carved surface.

MATERIAL   Limestone of uniform texture, flawed only by a fissure near the top.

SHAPE   Parallel sides with a nearly flat top. The front of the shaft is slightly narrower than the back. On either side four cord-holders have been drilled at intervals along the rear edge, passing through to the back.

DIMENSIONS	HLC	3.72	m
	EPB	0.38	m plus
	MW	2.04	m
	WBC	2.01	m
	MTh	0.39	m
	Rel	4.6	cm

CARVED AREAS   Front only.

PHOTOGRAPH   Graham, 1978.

DRAWING   Graham, based on detail photographs and field drawings of the lower half of the stela and all the inscriptions. Through ill luck, Maudslay's plaster cast in the British Museum could not be studied when this volume was in preparation because it was hidden behind the display panels of a temporary exhibition.

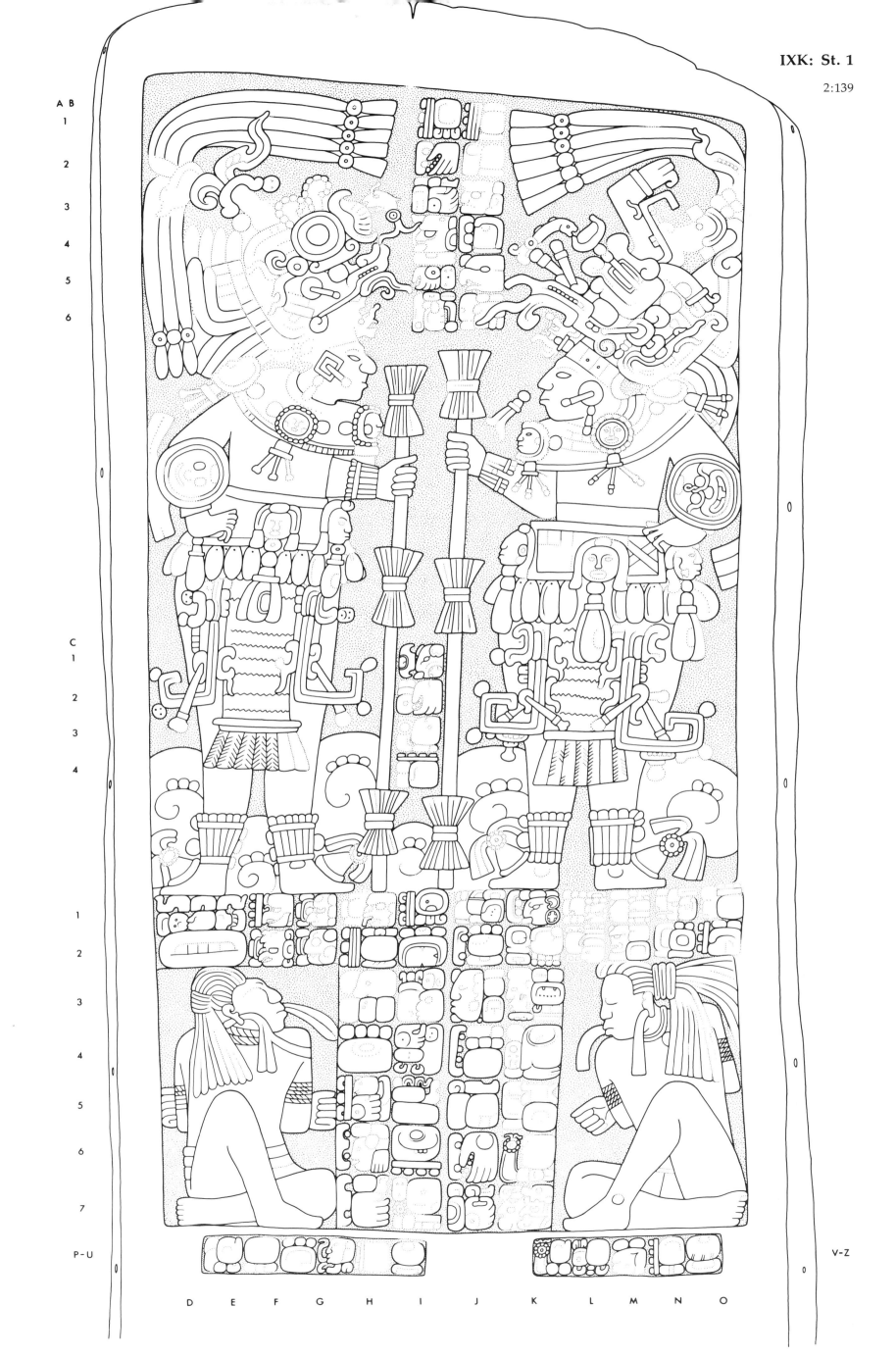

Ixkun, Stela 2

LOCATION   When Maudslay visited the site, this stela was already lying broken, with its sculptured face to the ground. It had been set directly in front of Structure 6, close to the foot of its stairway.

CONDITION   Broken into three large fragments and at least ten smaller ones. Morley reported that the butt, with the bottom row of glyphs, was still in situ; it has since been dug out. The carved surface, in fairly good condition when examined by Morley, has not deteriorated significantly since then. Three of the smaller fragments shown in Morley's photograph (carrying parts of glyphs A7 and A8) I

was unable to find in 1971; on the other hand I did find a small fragment constituting the lower edge of glyph B11 and the upper portion of B12, which had eluded him.

MATERIAL   Limestone.

SHAPE   Parallel sides, with poorly trimmed (or damaged) slanting top.

DIMENSIONS

HLC	2.14	m
PB	0.78	m
MW	1.06	m
WBC	1.03	m
MTh	0.33	m
Rel	0.9	cm

CARVED AREAS   Front only.

PHOTOGRAPH   Graham, 1971; portions of Morley's 1914 photograph that show the fragments not found in 1971 have been incorporated. The small photographs reproduced in the Introduction (p. 1:12) show glyph C3 of this stela.

DRAWING   Graham, based on a field drawing corrected by artificial light.

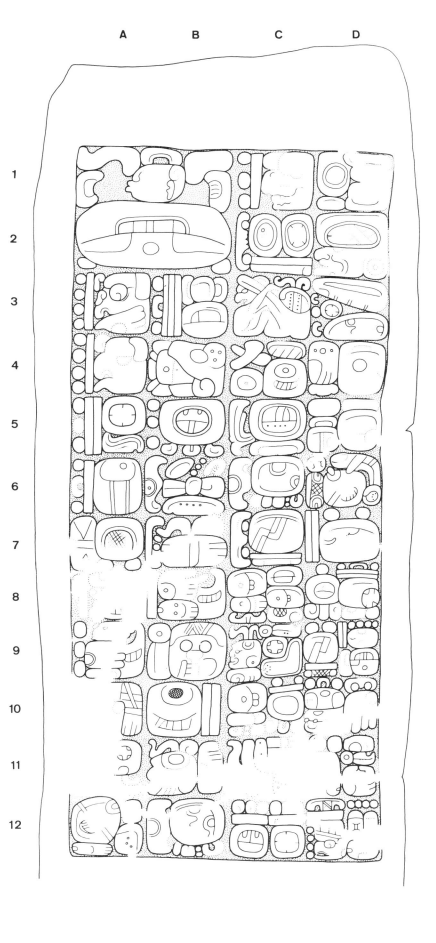

Ixkun, Stela 3

LOCATION   Lying with its carved face
up, in front of Structure 6 and just to
the south of Stela 2. Apparently seen
by Maudslay, it was first described by
Morley.

CONDITION   Only the upper half of this
stela survives, and its carved surface is
badly weathered. Removal of soil down
to the level of the plaza floor failed to dis-
close other fragments or the butt of the
stela.

MATERIAL   Limestone.

SHAPE   Parallel sides with a flattish top,
slightly rounded. The back of the shaft,
which is smoothly dressed, is narrower
than the front.

DIMENSIONS   Ht   2.56 m plus
             MW   1.08 m
             MTh   0.43 m
             Rel   4.0   cm

CARVED AREAS   Front only.

PHOTOGRAPH   Graham, 1978.

DRAWING   Graham.

Ixkun, Altar of Stela 3

LOCATION   Found by Graham to the west of Stela 3, buried below accumulated soil. It lay within 0.60 m of the broken lower edge of the stela, set in a floor of water-worn pebbles with its upper surface standing 10 cm above the level of that floor. The inscription appears to be oriented so as to read correctly for an observer facing west, with his back to the temple mound.

CONDITION   Two fragments are cracked from the main portion of the altar, but remain in place; another fragment is missing. The surface shows considerable erosion.

MATERIAL   Coarse limestone with shell inclusions, one of which adds spurious detail to the postfix at the right-hand side of glyph B1. A similar inclusion in the right-hand border of Stela 3, visible in the photograph, may be evidence of like origin.

SHAPE   Roughly oval, and poorly trimmed.

DIMENSIONS   Dia
(vert.) 1.00 m
Dia
(hor.) 1.32 m
MTh   0.27 m
Rel   1.7 cm

CARVED AREAS   Upper surface only.

PHOTOGRAPH   Graham, 1978.

DRAWING   Graham, based on a field drawing corrected by artificial light.

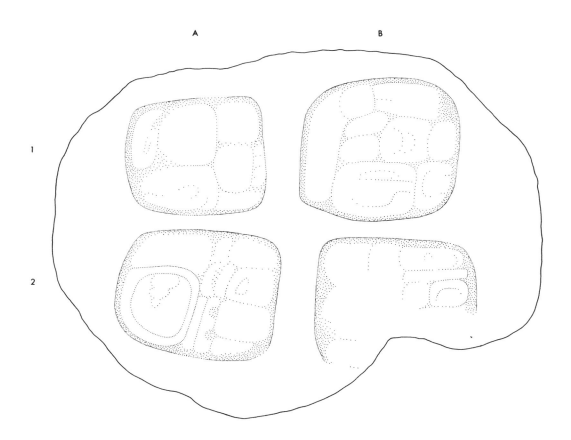

Ixkun, Stela 4

LOCATION   This stela was seen by Maudslay, already lying fallen on the west side of Structure 13 with its carved side up. It has not been moved since then.

CONDITION   The stela is broken off near the bottom of the lower panel of carving. No trace of the missing design can be retrieved from the fragments lying close to the butt, which is still in situ. The carved surface has suffered considerable, but uniform, erosion; it is also marred by several deep fissures. The upper right-hand corner is broken off and lost.

MATERIAL   Hard and fine-grained limestone.

SHAPE   A narrow shaft tapering slightly toward the bottom, with a rounded top.

DIMENSIONS   HLC   4.00 m plus
PB   unknown
MW   1.16 m
WBC   unknown
MTh   not recorded
Rel   2.7   cm

CARVED AREAS   Front only.

PHOTOGRAPH   Graham, 1971.

DRAWING   Graham, based on a field drawing corrected by artificial light.

IXK: St. 4

2:148

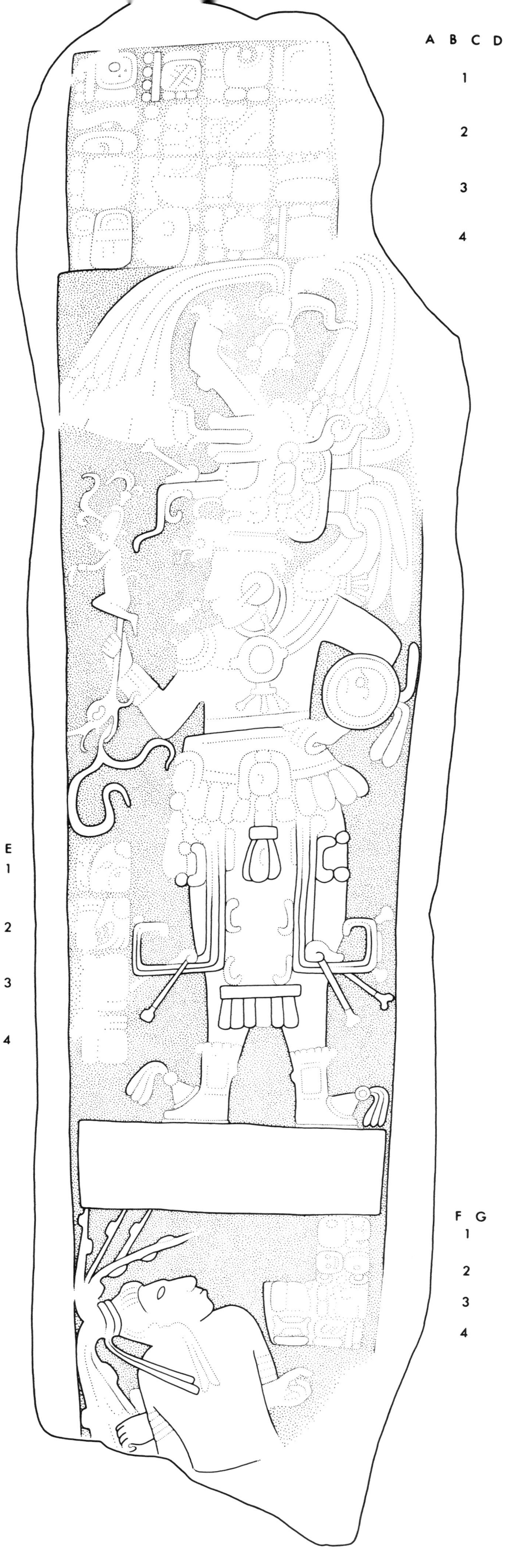

A B C D

1

2

3

4

E
1

2

3

4

F G
1

2

3

4

Ixkun, Stela 5

LOCATION   The stela was found in 1852 by Colonel Modesto Méndez and the artist Eusebio Lara, who made an unpublished drawing of it. It stood on an elevated platform at the terminus of the causeway that leads southward from the site center. No altar was closely associated with it. In 1972 the stela was broken up by a looter who removed many, but not all, of the fragments. The remainder were taken by me to the *alcaldía* in Dolores, whence they may have been removed by the Instituto de Antropología e Historia.

CONDITION   Before its destruction the stela was in fair condition, the most eroded area being the upper panel of hieroglyphs. Reduction of the shaft to portable fragments was evidently accomplished by building a fire round it, and then perhaps, once it was hot, dousing it with water.

MATERIAL   Hard, white limestone.

SHAPE   A very poorly trimmed shaft of roughly rectangular shape. The carved surface was by no means flat.

DIMENSIONS   HLC   2.65 m
PB   0.75 m approx.
MW   1.00 m
WBC   1.00 m
MTh   0.26 m
Rel   1.0   cm

CARVED AREAS   Front only.

PHOTOGRAPHS   Morley, 1914; the very top of the stela, missing from Morley's photograph, has been supplied by Graham.

DRAWING   Graham, traced from a properly aligned but otherwise poor photograph taken by him and based, as to details, on a field drawing corrected by artificial light.

Detail

Ucanal and Yaltutu

A NOTE ON THE NAMES   In his field notebooks (Peabody Museum Archives) R.E. Merwin, the first to describe both these sites, employed in some places the form Yokanal, and in others Ucanal, the latter being the form universally adopted since. As to Yaltutu, this spelling of a name that is applied to several places in Peten (see the Introduction to this work, p. 1:11) is the one being used in preference to Yaltitud, the version proposed and employed by Morley. Since deciding to make this change, I have found that Merwin wrote Yaltutu, or sometimes Yaltatu, in his field notes. As this very small site is clearly an outlying part of Ucanal, the two sites will be described together.

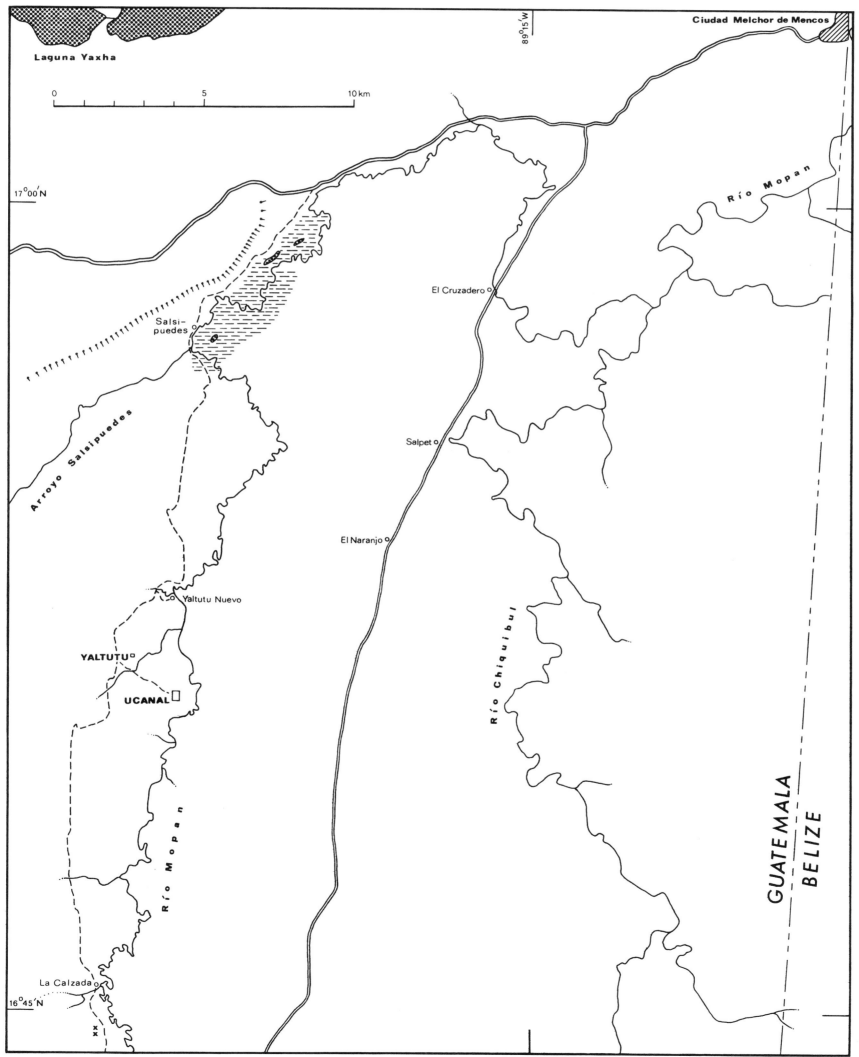

Both sites lie near the west bank of the Mopan River, just below a double bend in its course; Ucanal lies within the elbow formed by the lower bend. The high ground on which the ruins stand is the southwestern extremity of a spur of hills ranging up to 400 m above sea level that intrudes into the otherwise rather flat basin through which the Mopan and Salsipuedes rivers flow in this region. In the channel that it has cut through these hills, the Mopan cascades over a number of rock ledges. Even below these, the river cannot be classed as navigable.

One feasible route to these ruins is from the north, as shown on the area map. The route is difficult, however, because the Salsipuedes River must be crossed, as well as an area of low ground that is flooded during the rains. Once these obstacles are overcome, the old lumber road passes through flat and sometimes stony ground, much of it *corozal.* Conditions on the high ground surrounding the ruins are reported to have changed since my last visit, as farmers have moved into the area.

Another approach to the ruins, which I took in 1972, was along a trail passing through El Cruzadero, Naranjo, and Grano de Oro, and over to a shallow crossing place on the Mopan River at La Calzada; thence north to Ucanal. In recent years a road has been built that follows a rather similar — and over some of its length an identical — route, but its course as shown on the area map, transferred from a semiofficial Guatemalan map, may not be accurate. The large new village, Calzada Mopan, is shown on that map about 8 km south of the position I calculate, perhaps erroneously, for the old *caserío* La Calzada. In any case, this road, which connects with the Flores–Poptun road at Sabaneta, may in future provide the best initial approach to Ucanal and Yaltutu.

PRINCIPAL INVESTIGATIONS AT THE SITES

Merwin, working for the Peabody Museum, Harvard University, made his visit to Ucanal and Yaltutu in 1914; while there he mapped the sites and photographed some of the monuments, later writing a report which remains

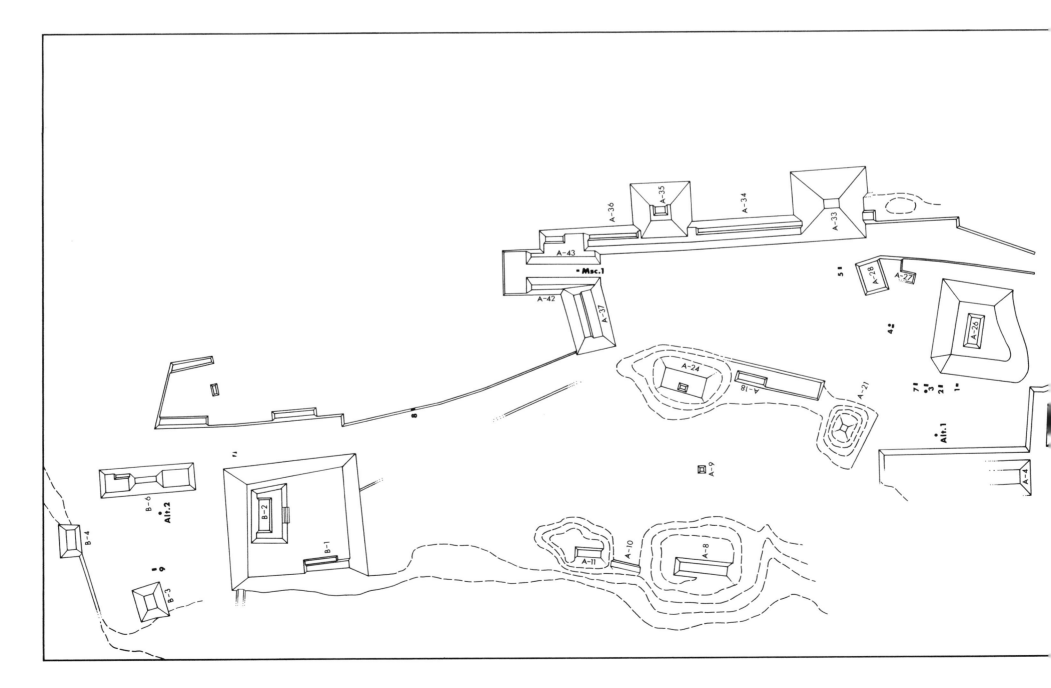

unpublished. A month after Merwin's visit, Morley spent one day at the sites examining monuments. Merwin's material was later used by Morley for his own report (1937–38, vol. 2, pp. 186–204).

My own first attempt to locate these sites, in 1967, was hampered by the oblivion into which they seemed to have fallen locally, largely because of the absence of lumbering or *chiclero* activity and the tangled state in which the forest was left by the hurricane of 1961. This oblivion, however, was not complete, as became apparent when Yaltutu was at last located: Stela 1 was discovered to have been cut up by looters a very short time before. Ucanal, on the other hand, which I did not succeed in finding until 1972, remained at that time quite untouched.

Shortly after rediscovering Ucanal, I returned to make the site plan published here, record the monuments, and remove Stela 4 and the two carved altars to safety.

NOTES ON THE RUINS
The ceremonial area centers on a plaza of irregular shape, bounded by Structures A-26, A-33, A-35, A-24, and A-21, the two last named being adaptations of hillocks. Within this area are eight carved monuments. Another sculpture, Miscellaneous 1, was found in 1972 on the center line of the ball court at the northern extremity of the plaza (Structures A-42 and A-43), and this can only have come to be there as the result of Postclassic — or even post-Conquest — activity. On the grounds of epigraphic content, style, dimensions, shape, and type of stone, this piece can identified with certainty as a displaced member of the Naranjo Hieroglyphic Stairway. As such, it has already been published in part two of this volume (pp. 2:107 and 2:110).

It may be worth recording here that the ground on which the stone lay face up was quite flat and undisturbed by tree falls, and the level of the soil surface directly beneath it was some 5 cm below that of the surrounding surface. A small excavation revealed a soil accumulation of 20 cm beneath the stone, overlying a floor of stone chips and decayed plaster.

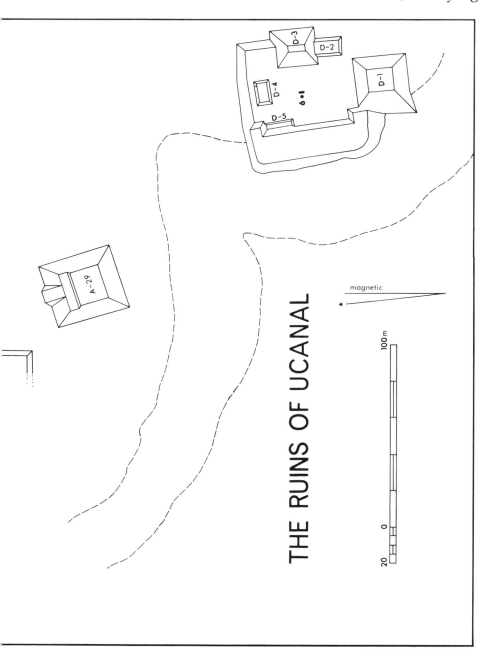

THE RUINS OF UCANAL

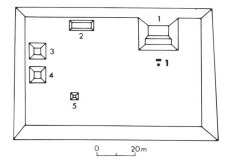

SKETCH PLAN OF YALTUTU

Near the southeast corner of the main plaza a causeway runs from in front of Structure A-33 toward the south for 90 m before terminating abruptly.

From the northwest corner of the plaza another causeway leads in a direction somewhat west of north to a small plaza containing Stela 9 and Altar 2, both plain. The fallen stela is 2.2 m long, 0.77 m wide, and 0.49 m thick; the altar 0.74 m in diameter and 0.31 m thick. East of this group, designated by Morley as Group B, and northeast of Group A, a number of mounds are shown on Merwin's plan (published by Morley) as constituting Group C, in which three plain stelae are also marked.

To the north and west of Group B the terrain falls away gently, while to the west of Group A it becomes broken, with several of the natural eminences having had structures built on them.

Lying at the same distance from the main plaza as Group B, and in the opposite direction, there is found Group D, a small acropolis in the center of which Stela 6 and its altar were set.

The trail from our campsite on the river bank went uphill in a more or less northerly direction for a distance of 400 or 500 m until reaching the west side of Structure A-29. At the side of the trail, some 150 m along the way, there was a ring of roughly circular flat stones, the diameter of the ring being about 7 m.

In searching for Yaltutu, several mounds of some size were seen, most of them on the southeast side of the arroyo marked on the map as separating Yaltutu from Ucanal, and therefore clearly outlying elements of the latter. Although Yaltutu was the only mound of any size seen on the other side of the arroyo, others may well exist.

A NOTE ON THE PLAN OF THE SITE   The plan of Ucanal reproduced here is the result of my incomplete survey of 1972. Many structures outside the central area that were plotted by Merwin were neither surveyed nor even visited by me, nor have they been transferred to my plan from Merwin's, since the latter is revealed as rather too inaccurate for the purpose. In addition to the three plain stelae in Group C already mentioned (C1 and C3), several other stelae designated by Morley as A1 to A5, and D1 are likewise missing from the plan. The existence of Stela B2 is doubted.

In accordance with the general policy of numbering carved and uncarved stelae in a single series, Morley's Stela B1 has been redesignated as Stela 9. Stela 8, not shown by Merwin, also seems to have been plain. As far as possible, structure numbers have been left unchanged.

The plan of Yaltutu is taken from Morley's version (1937–38, vol. 2, fig. 33) of Merwin's plan, modified to incorporate the few measurements I took.

REGISTER OF INSCRIPTIONS   At Ucanal: Stelae 2-4, 6, 7
Altar of Stela 3
Altar 1
Miscellaneous 1 (see Note 3)
At Yaltutu: Stela 1

NOTES   1. Stela 1 appears to be a zoomorph, 2.00 m long, 1.20 m wide, and 0.55 m high. It is severely eroded.
2. Stela 5 is broken in half and badly eroded. It may have depicted a personage facing proper right, holding a lance, and standing with feet apart on a prostrate captive. Its dimensions are: HLC ca. 2.85 m, PB 0.86 m, MW 1.44 m, MTh 0.53 m, Rel ca. 3.5 cm.
3. For Miscellaneous 1 (Naranjo, Hieroglyphic Stairway 1, Block XIII), see above and part two of this volume, pp. 2:107 and 2:110.

REFERENCE CITED   MORLEY, SYLVANUS G.
1937–38   *The Inscriptions of Peten.* Carnegie Institution of Washington, Publication 437, 5 vols. Washington, D.C.

Ucanal, Stela 2

LOCATION   Found by Merwin lying with its sculptured face up, the second from the southern end of a line of four monuments on the west side of Structure A-26.

CONDITION   As noted by Merwin and Morley, the carving on this stela seems to have been left unfinished. The surface has suffered considerable erosion, and part of the surface at the upper right-hand corner and on both sides lower down has split away at a bedding plane, and could not be found.

MATERIAL   Fine-grained limestone of pronounced laminar structure.

SHAPE   Parallel sides, with rounded top. The butt is somewhat pointed.

DIMENSIONS   Ht   3.79 m
             MW   1.07 m
             MTh   0.44 m
             Rel   4.0   cm

CARVED AREAS   Front only.

PHOTOGRAPH   Graham, 1972.

DRAWING   Graham, based on photographs and a field drawing of the inscription.

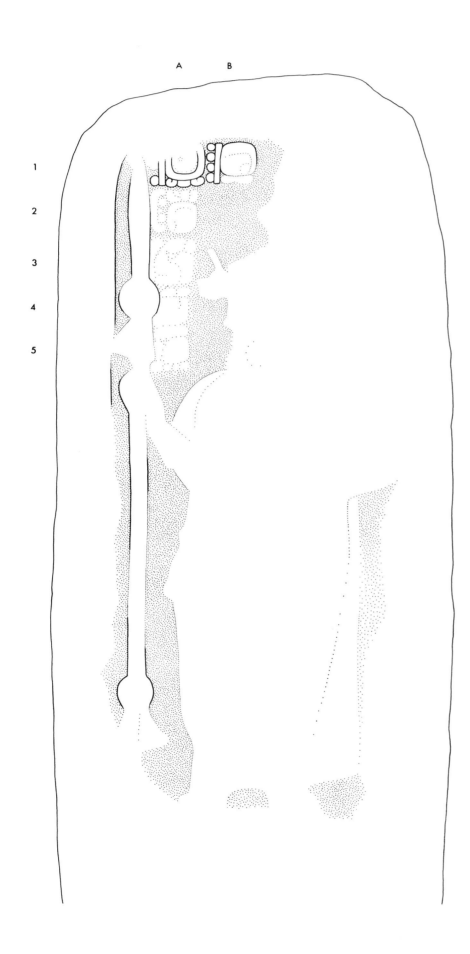

Ucanal, Stela 3

LOCATION   Found by Merwin lying with its sculptured face up. It is the second from the northern end of a line of four monuments on the west side of Structure A-26. A sculptured altar is associated with it.

CONDITION   Unbroken; its carved surface is quite badly eroded.

MATERIAL   Limestone.

SHAPE   Tapers slightly toward the top, which is nearly flat.

DIMENSIONS   HLC   2.55 m
PB   2.00 m
MW   1.61 m
WBC   1.61 m
MTh   0.57 m
Rel   7.0 cm

CARVED AREAS   Front surface only.

PHOTOGRAPH   Graham, 1972.

DRAWING   Graham, based on a field drawing corrected by artificial light.

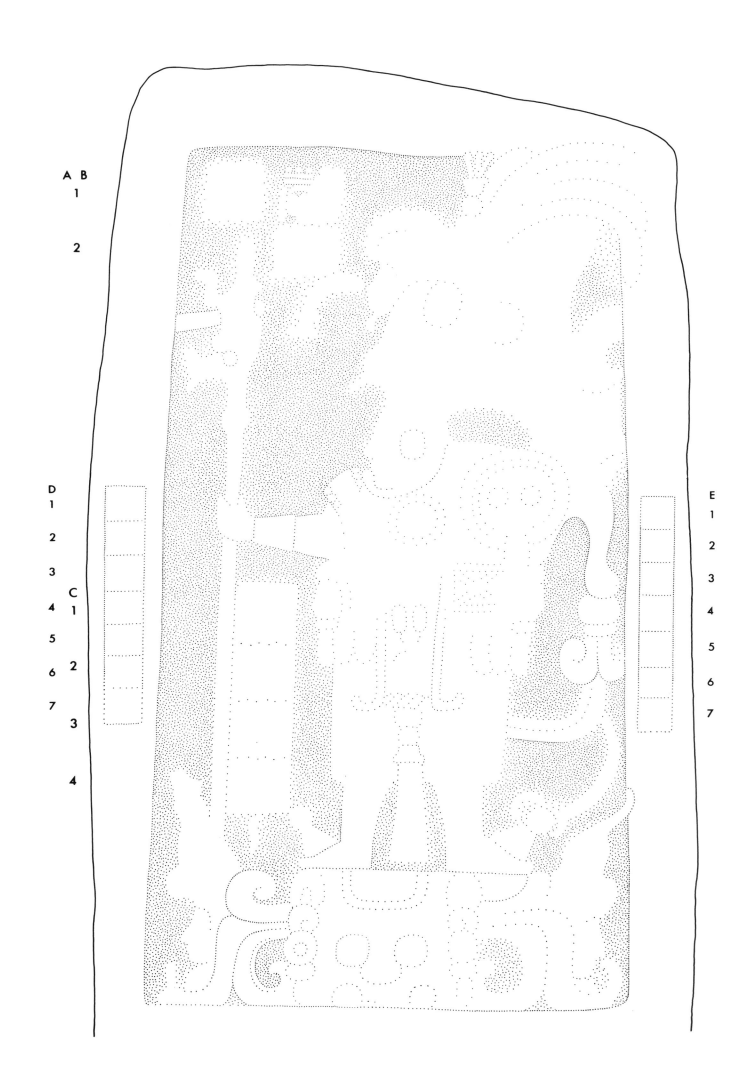

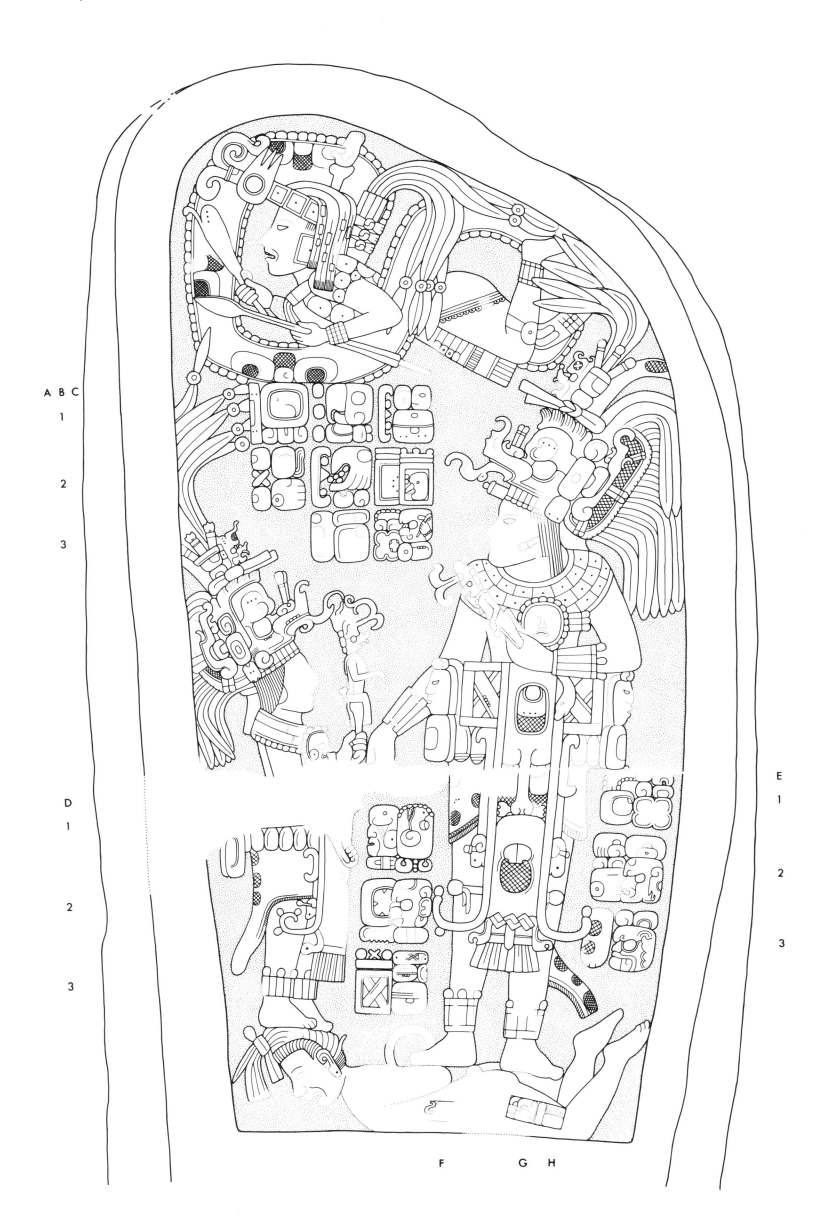

UCN: St. 4

LOCATION   Merwin found the stela, about 20 m north of Structure A-26. It was broken in half, with the lower part apparently still in situ but tilted forward. An incomplete circular altar about 0.95 m in diameter and 0.38 m thick was associated with the stela. In 1972, using funds provided by La Asociación Tikal, I removed the stela to the Museo Nacional de Arqueología y Etnología, Guatemala City.

CONDITION   Broken in two when found, and now repaired. There is a small loss extending along the left-hand half of the fracture. The carved surface is for the most part in excellent condition. A filling of plaster survives in a few cavities in the carved surface.

MATERIAL   Hard grayish white limestone, flawed by numerous small cavities.

SHAPE   The sculptured surface is flat, and narrower than the back of the shaft. The top is peaked unsymmetrically; the sides taper toward the bottom.

DIMENSIONS

HLC	1.90	m
PB	0.65	m
MW	1.07	m (front)
WBC	0.93	m
MTh	0.53	m
Rel	2.1	cm

CARVED AREAS   Front only.

PHOTOGRAPH   Graham, 1975.

DRAWING   Graham, based on a field drawing corrected by artificial light.

Ucanal, Stela 6

LOCATION   Found by Merwin on the west side of Structure D-3, in the center of a small court. The associated altar, now in several pieces, has a diameter of about 1.75 m, and a thickness of 0.40 m.

CONDITION   Broken below the base of carving, with part of the butt still in the ground. The sculptured surface is severely eroded, especially over the lower part of the monument.

MATERIAL   Limestone.

SHAPE   The sides taper toward the top, which may have been nearly flat.

DIMENSIONS   HLC   2.71 m approx.
PB   0.86 m plus
MW   1.50 m *
WBC   1.41 m
MTh   0.60 m
Rel   5.0   cm appprox.

CARVED AREAS   Front only.

PHOTOGRAPHS   Graham, 1972.

DRAWING   Graham, based on a field drawing corrected by artificial light.

* Below the base of carving

Stereophotos

Ucanal, Stela 7

LOCATION   Found by Graham lying with its sculptured face up, the northernmost in a line of four monuments on the west side of Structure A-26.

CONDITION   The stela is broken into four pieces, and its entire sculptured surface is severely eroded. Not a single hieroglyph is legible.

MATERIAL   Limestone.

SHAPE   Parallel sides, with a nearly flat top.

DIMENSIONS

HLC	1.92	m
PB	1.28	m
MW	1.46	m
WBC	1.46	m
MTh	0.35	m
Rel	2.5	cm

CARVED AREAS   Front only.

PHOTOGRAPH   Graham, 1972.

LOCATION   Found by Graham tilted up by the roots of a fallen tree on the east side of Structure A-4. It was removed to Tikal for safekeeping in 1972.

CONDITION   The stone has lost two segments by fracture at either side, and the carved surface has suffered considerable erosion.

SHAPE   Originally, perhaps nearly circular.

DIMENSIONS   Dia   1.30 m approx.
                MTh   0.26 m
                Rel   1.2   cm

CARVED AREAS   Upper surface only.

PHOTOGRAPH   Graham, 1972.

DRAWING   Graham, based on a field drawing corrected by artificial light.

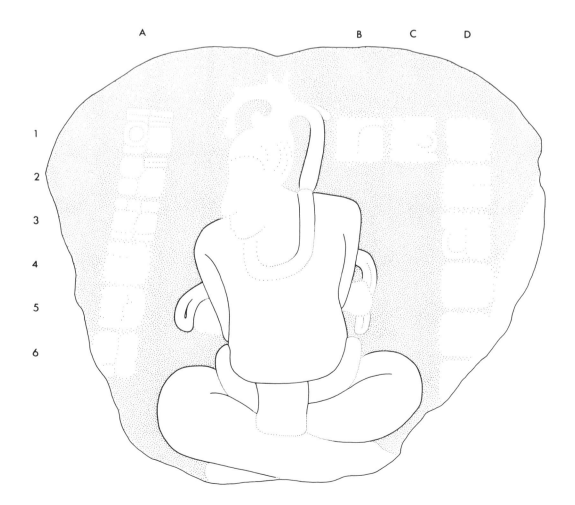

Ucanal, Altar of Stela 3

LOCATION Found by Merwin lying about 3 m in front of Stela 3. In 1972 it was removed to the Museo Nacional de Arqueología y Etnología, Guatemala City.

CONDITION Intact, but considerably eroded.

MATERIAL Fine-grained limestone.

SHAPE Nearly circular.

DIMENSIONS
HLC (vert.) 1.58 m
HLC (hor.) 1.67 m
MTh 0.52 m
Rel 4.0 cm

CARVED AREAS Upper surface only.

PHOTOGRAPHS Entire surface: Merwin, 1914. Stereophotos: Graham.

DRAWING Graham, based on a field drawing corrected by artificial light.

Stereophotos

Yaltutu, Stela 1

LOCATION   Unbroken and erect when found by Merwin. The stela stood on the south side of Structure 1, about 6 m from its foot. In front of the stela was a circular altar 0.74 m in diameter and 0.28 m thick. The front of the stela, which had been cut off by looters in 1966 and taken to Belize, was later confiscated and returned to Guatemala. It is preserved in the Museo Nacional de Arqueología y Etnología.

CONDITION   The stela has lost all fine detail from the effects of erosion on a stone of nonuniform texture. The front of the stela has been sawn into pieces about 10 cm thick, from which small portions have broken off and are missing, among them one carrying glyph A2.

MATERIAL   Limestone; a recemented fault breccia.

SHAPE   Parallel sides, with a rounded top.

DIMENSIONS   HLC   1.72 m
PB   0.80 m
MW   1.00 m
WBC   0.98 m
MTh   0.69 m
Rel   5.0   cm

CARVED AREAS   Front only.

PHOTOGRAPH   Merwin, printed from his original negative.

DRAWING   Graham, based on a drawing of the reassembled fragments.

Ixtutz

LOCATION AND ACCESS

The ruins lie some 8 km southeast of Dolores, in southeastern Peten. Two trails lead to them from the Flores–Poptun road. One trail passes through La Borrachera, an abandoned house site named for some forgotten event, and distinguished besides by having a well in the form of a hole 2 m in diameter, dug down through mud and stones to water at a depth of 3 m. The other route skirts a large mound (marked x on the area map) built upon a high terrace. I have not examined this mound.

The ruins are found in a small flat area surrounded by hills typical of a karst zone. Structures 26 to 35 are built on one of these hills. Apart from the well already mentioned, other sources of water are the *aguada* (not always dependable) shown at the northeast corner of the site plan and another lying between Structures 20 and 21, which collects water only during the rainy season.

PRINCIPAL INVESTIGATIONS AT THE SITE

The first published mention of this site resulted from the visit of Colonel Modesto Méndez and Eusebio Lara in 1852. In a report published in a German journal (Ritter 1853) "Yxtutz" is stated to be south of Dolores, and two of the stelae, numbers 1 and 3, are illustrated in somewhat fanciful drawings, but little other information is given. Following Méndez and Lara's visit, the ruins relapsed into oblivion for more than a century; then in 1970 a Maya who farmed milpa land nearby brought Merle Greene Robertson to the site. She revisited the site twice in the following year to make rubbings of the sculpture and to map the site, soon afterward publishing a report on it (Robertson 1972).

Having been told by her of Ixtutz, von Euw and I visited it in 1972. Von Euw, who preceded me to the site by a few days, began his work by transporting the blocks of the mosaic wall panel (Panel 1) by pack mule to Dolores. Following my arrival, we made our own plan of the site and recorded the monuments, including Stela 4, which we found to be carved on the underside. Considering this stela also worth rescuing, we engaged men to cut a roadway to the savanna flanking the Flores highway, and achieved our purpose with a truck provided by the Guatemalan army.

NOTES ON THE RUINS

Ixtutz has a clearly defined main plaza bounded by the largest structures of the site where all the sculptured monuments are found. Also within the plaza is one plain stela, the fallen Stela 5 (original height ca. 2.25 m, MW 0.75 m, MTh 0.27 m). One of these structures, number 2, is clearly an adaptation of a natural feature; the rest may have been constructed on level ground. On top of Structure 2 there is a well-preserved platform 0.70 m high, built of neatly cut stones of varied sizes and shapes. Any building supported by this platform could only have been of perishable materials.

The level, and probably at one time plaster-floored, ceremonial plaza area has an extension toward the northeast that forms an enclosed precinct having some of the character of a causeway. With it are associated a small plaza group and a *plazuela*.

From the northwest corner of the main plaza a short causeway, or ceremonial way, bounded by very low walls, leads to the foot of a hill that rises to a height of 45 m. At its foot, above a wide step that seems to terminate the causeway, stands a stone shaft, set diagonally, the sides of which measure about 1.0 m by 1.1 m. Since this may have been set up for ceremonial purposes it is marked on the plan as Stela 6.

NOTES ON THE PLAN OF THE SITE

The density of undergrowth found at this site at the time of our visit (due to the destructive hurricane of 1961) made surveying more difficult than usual. For this reason, perhaps, there is some lack of agreement between Merle Greene Robertson's plan and ours, especially in the area lying between the causeway that runs to the foot of the hill and a line joining our Structures 21 and 22 (a renumbering of structures for our plan was unavoidable). Robertson also shows a group of four mounds on a common platform south of our Structure 25, which we missed.

A symbol employed in the plan but not shown in the table of site plan symbols (p. 1:26) needs to be explained. A line punctuated by small sawteeth denotes a single step in isolation, such as might be found between two plaza areas of different level, or one edge of a low and broad causeway wall. The sawtooth element was inspired by the generally triangular shape of the stones often used by the Maya to form such features. Thus the sawteeth point toward the higher level.

REGISTER OF INSCRIPTIONS AT IXTUTZ   Stelae 1-4
Panel 1

REFERENCES CITED   RITTER, CARL
1853   "Ueber neue Entdeckungen und Beobachtungen in Guatemala und Yuca-
tan," *Zeitschrift,* Gesellschaft für Erdkunde zu Berlin, vol. 1, pp. 161–193.
Berlin.
ROBERTSON, MERLE GREENE
1972   "Notes on the Ruins of Ixtutz, Southeastern Peten" (with an Appendix by
John A. Graham), *Contributions of the University of California Archaeological
Research Facility,* no. 16, pp. 89–104. Berkeley.

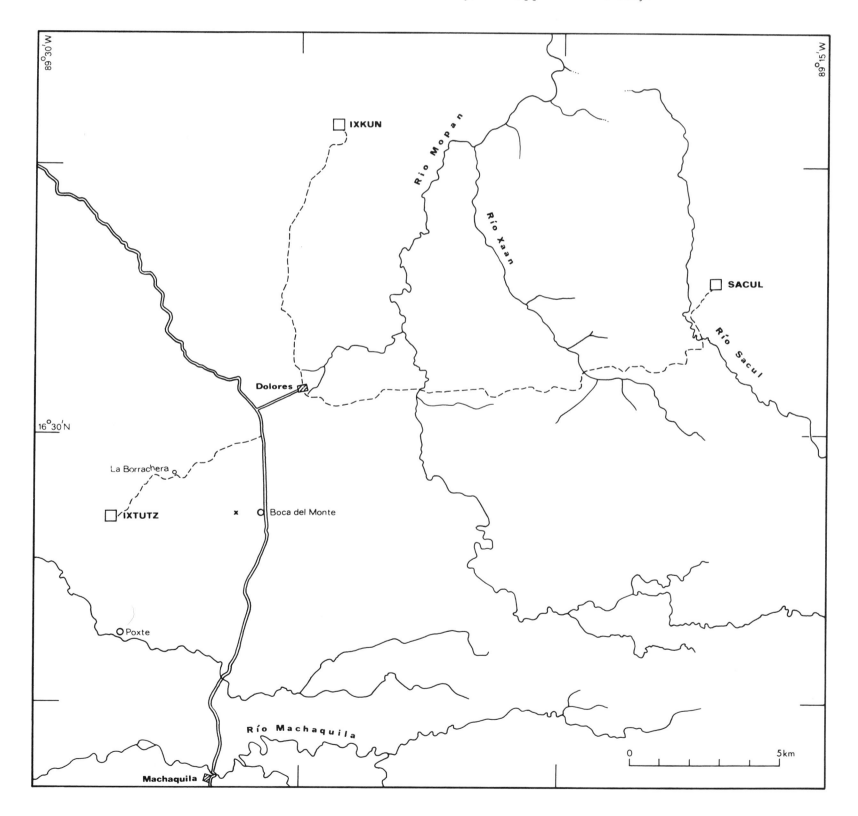

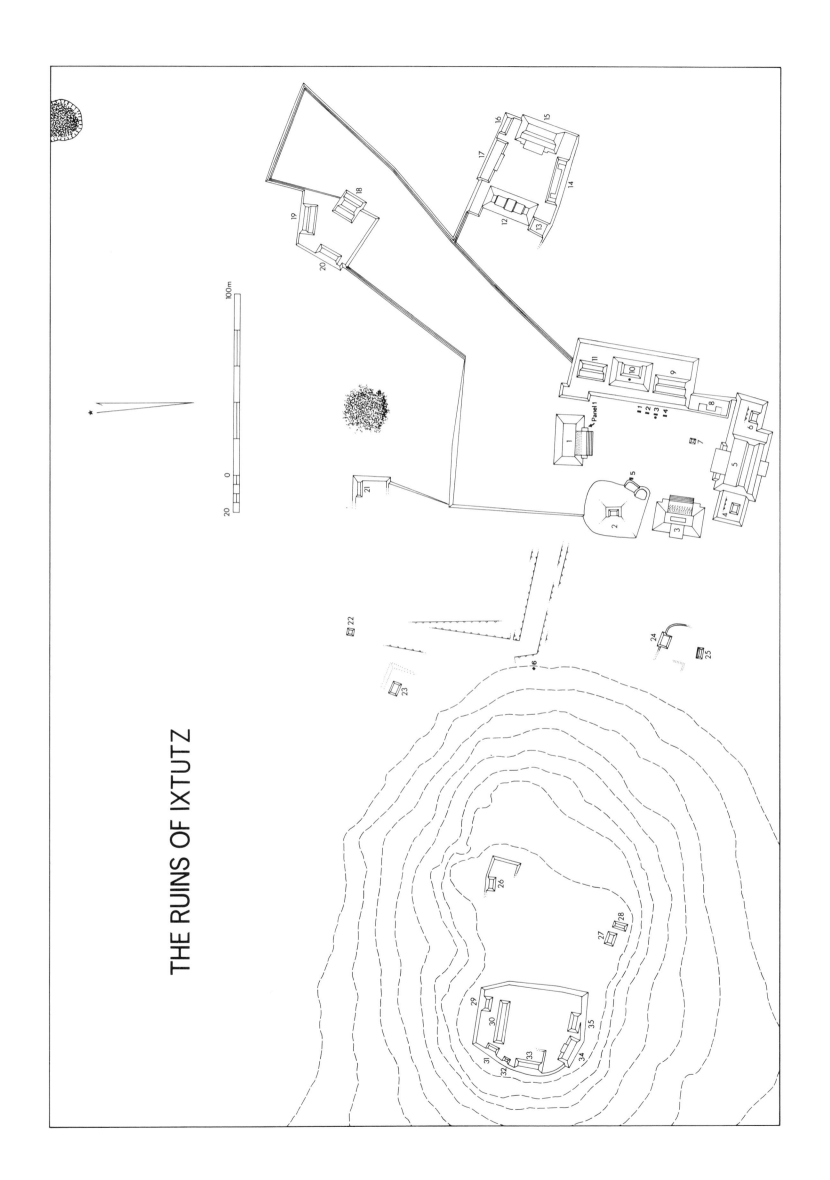

THE RUINS OF IXTUTZ

Ixtutz, Stela 1

LOCATION   Still standing, the stela is the northernmost in a line of four stelae on the west side of the platform on which Structures 9, 10, and 11 are built. It was first reported by Modesto Méndez.

CONDITION   Intact, but severely eroded.

MATERIAL   Limestone.

SHAPE   A poorly fashioned shaft, flat-topped, with approximately parallel sides.

DIMENSIONS
HLC	2.36	m
PB	unknown	
MW	1.11	m
WBC	0.94	m
MTh	0.38	m
Rel	0.6	cm

CARVED AREAS   Front only.

PHOTOGRAPH   Graham, 1972.

DRAWING   Graham, based on a field drawing corrected by artificial light.

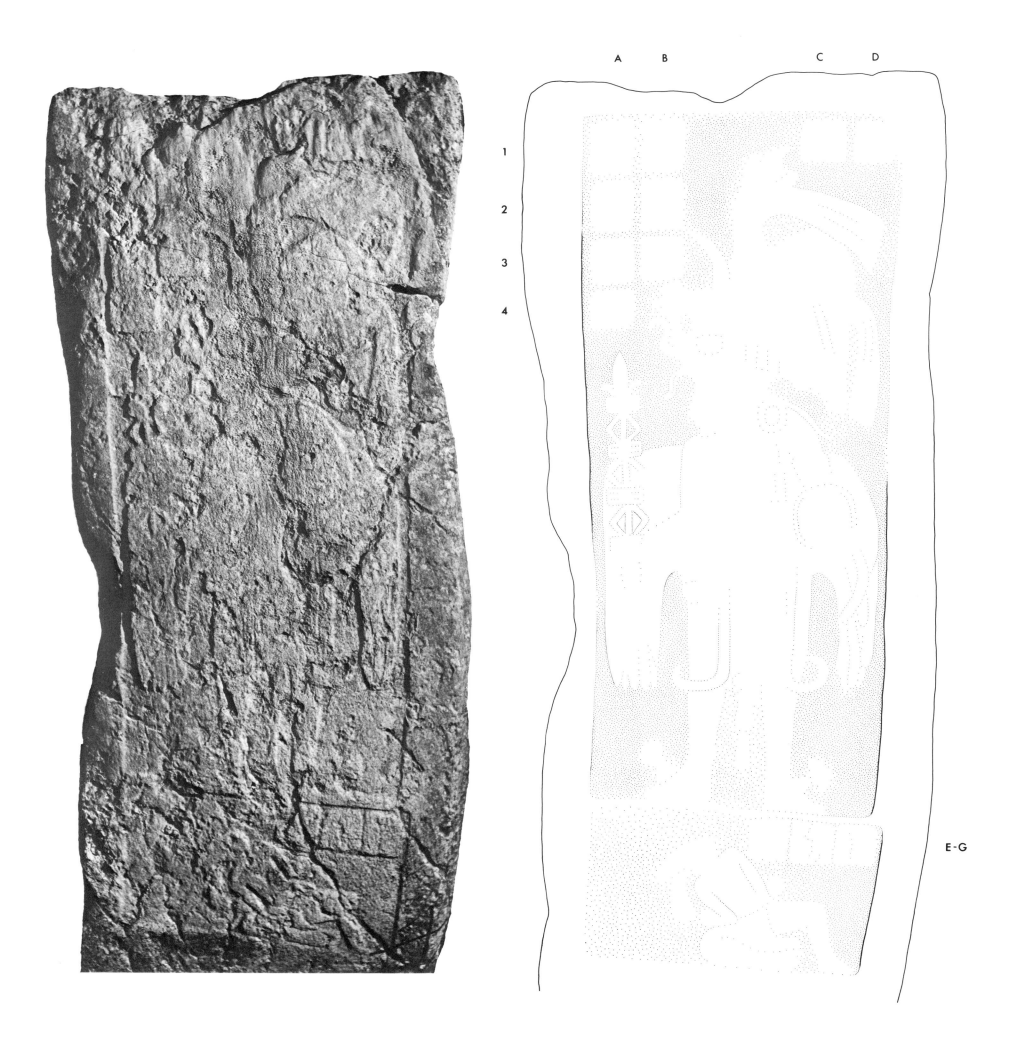

Ixtutz, Stela 2

LOCATION   Second from the northern end of four stelae on the western side of the platform on which Structures 9, 10, and 11 are built. The stela lies on its back with the butt still in situ, as it did when first reported by Merle Greene Robertson.

CONDITION   Broken into three extant pieces: the main body of the shaft, one small fragment, and the butt carrying a small portion of the design. Other small fragments are lost. A vertical fissure runs down the middle of the sculptured face, the surface of which is severely eroded.

MATERIAL   Limestone.

SHAPE   Tapers slightly toward the bottom; the top is flat.

DIMENSIONS   HLC   2.77 m
             PB   unknown
             MW   1.40 m
             WBC   1.17 m approx.
             MTh   0.38 m
             Rel   1.7   cm

CARVED AREAS   Front only.

PHOTOGRAPH   Graham, 1972.

DRAWING   Graham, based on a field drawing corrected by artificial light.

A B C D E F

G

1

2

3

4

5

6

7

8

9

(etc.)

H

1 – ?

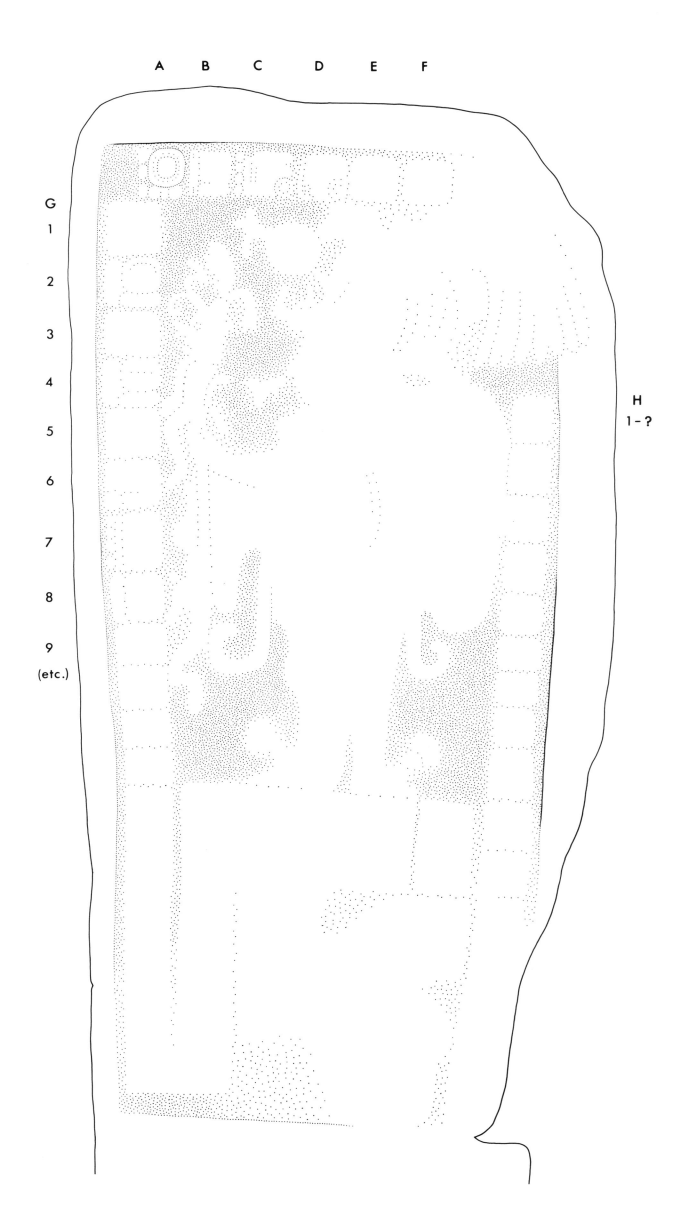

LOCATION   The stela lies broken with its carved face up, the second from the southern end in a line of four stelae on the west side of the platform on which Structures 9, 10, and 11 are built. As Lara attempted to draw the stela, it may be that the stela was still erect in 1853. In front of this stela is a plain circular altar 1.55 m in diameter and 0.46 m thick.

CONDITION   The top of the shaft is broken into three fragments, and the butt is broken off at the base of carving. The surface is severely eroded.

MATERIAL   Limestone.

SHAPE   Slightly bulging sides, with a rounded top.

DIMENSIONS
HLC	2.80	m
PB	1.47	m
MW	1.16	m
WBC	1.06	m
MTh	0.27	m
Rel	4.5	cm

CARVED AREAS   Front only.

PHOTOGRAPH   Graham, 1972.

DRAWING   Graham, based on a field drawing corrected by artificial light.

Ixtutz, Stela 4

LOCATION Found lying on its face (i.e., fallen toward the west), the southernmost in a line of four stelae on the west side of the platform on which Structures 9, 10, and 11 are built. The stela was removed in 1972, first to Tikal, and later to the Museo Nacional de Arqueología y Etnología, Guatemala.

CONDITION Intact, except perhaps for the loss of the bottom of the butt. The upper part of the inscription is in almost pristine state, although lower down much of it has been lost through flaking.

MATERIAL Honey-colored limestone.

SHAPE Evidently intended to have a symmetrical, tapered shape, the shaft appears to have had a defective upper left-hand corner even before it was carved.

DIMENSIONS
HLC	1.83	m
PB	0.33	m plus
MW	1.16	m
WBC	1.02	m
MTh	0.40	m
Rel	1.0	cm

CARVED AREAS Front only.

PHOTOGRAPH Graham, 1972.

DRAWING Graham, based on a field drawing corrected by artificial light.

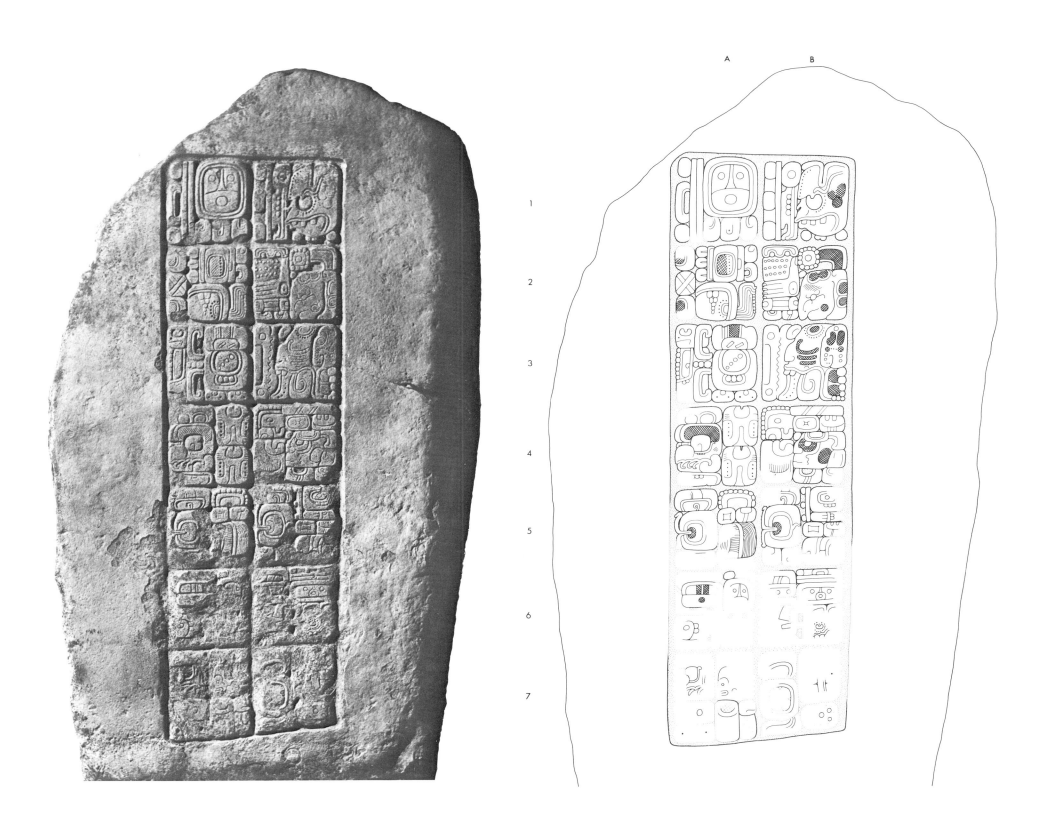

Ixtutz, Panel 1

LOCATION   The constituent blocks of this incomplete mosaic panel were found by Robertson among rubble on the south side of Structure 1, east of the stairway. Intending to remove them to safety by helicopter, she assembled all that could be found without excavation. Von Euw, however, took them to Dolores with pack mules. The blocks were then removed from Dolores by the Instituto de Antropología e Historia.

CONDITION   Many elements of the panel are missing, perhaps still buried in debris. Robertson (1972, p. 94) states that fifteen fragments were found; we have a record of eleven, some of which are in excellent condition, others broken or badly weathered.

MATERIAL   Limestone.

SHAPE   The undamaged blocks are rectangular and neatly trimmed.

DIMENSIONS   The width of the undamaged blocks varies between 0.29 and 0.37 m, the thickness between 0.20 and 0.50 m. The depth of relief runs up to 7.0 cm.

CARVED AREAS   One surface only.

PHOTOGRAPHS   Graham, 1972.

DRAWINGS   Graham, based on field
drawings corrected by artificial light.
Since no two of these blocks appear to
mate, the disposition of the blocks in the
photograph and drawing is to a large ex-
tent arbitrary, as is the numbering of
them in Roman numerals. The suggested
form of glyph-block designation of, for
example, the "up-ended frog" glyph on
Block VIII is IXZ: Pan. 1, VIII, 2.

Naranjo, Stela 41

LOCATION   Found on the west side of Structure C-10. This structure, 9 m high, and other smaller ones in front of it are situated on the flattened top of a hill which stands about 28 m higher than ground level in the plaza to the west of it. Neither Morley nor I ever ascended this hill while exploring the site, nor did either of us notice the parallel bounding walls of a ceremonial approach up the hillside. Early in 1978 looters who were cutting a trench into the mound came upon the stela, which apparently lay covered by rubble. Their activities were discovered before they had managed to remove the stela. Shortly thereafter it was removed to Melchor de Mencos by Marco Antonio Bailey of the Instituto de Antropología e Historia. The revised portion of the site plan printed on this page is based on a survey that I made in 1978.

CONDITION   Unbroken and rather well preserved, apart from areas near the bottom that have split off and the damaged top edge. The face was evidently obliterated in antiquity.

MATERIAL   Limestone.

SHAPE   Parallel sides, with a rounded top.

DIMENSIONS
HLC   1.45 m
PB   0.80 m
MW   0.76 m
WBC   0.71 m
MTh   0.40 m
Rel   1.5 cm

CARVED AREAS   Front only.

PHOTOGRAPH   Graham, 1978.

DRAWING   Graham, based on a field drawing corrected by artificial light.

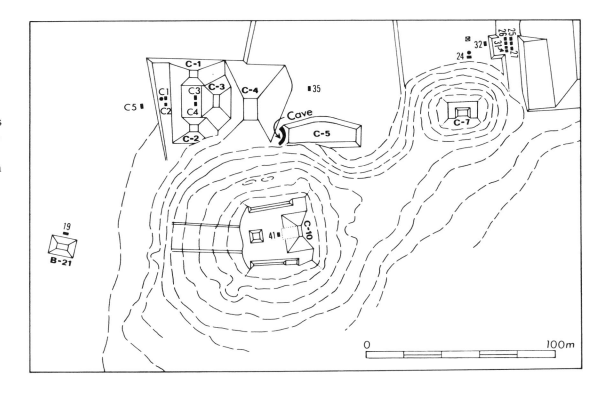

Naranjo, Ball-court Sculpture 1

LOCATION   When found in 1979 by site guards employed by the Instituto de Antropología e Historia, this fragment was lying on the ground to the northwest of Structures B-32 and B-33, a pair of mounds that forms one of the two ball courts at this site.

CONDITION   The fragment represents about one third of a ball-court marker ring. The side lying uppermost is so badly eroded that the two hieroglyphs carved on it are barely distinguishable; the other side and the periphery show only moderate weathering.

MATERIAL   White limestone.

SHAPE   A carefully dressed ring of square section with rounded inner edges. At one end the fragment becomes wider, where presumably a tenon was formed.

DIMENSIONS
Outer dia	0.42	m
Inner dia	0.19	m
MTh	0.20	m
Rel	0.4	cm

CARVED AREAS   Both sides and the periphery in intaglio or depressed relief.

PHOTOGRAPH   Graham, 1979.

DRAWING   Graham, based on a field drawing not checked by artificial light.

NOTE   A ring without surviving tenon was found by von Euw at Xultun, just to the north of Structures A-16 and A-17, a ball court. Its outer and inner diameters are 0.42 m and 0.12 m; its thickness 0.22 m.

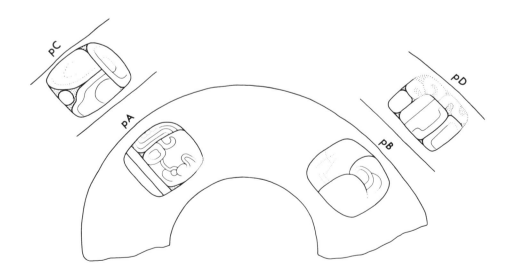